'These beautiful poems do the most important thing - they risk something. There is something heroic about Quill's utterly shameless love of language, brimming over, daring you to say that you've had your fill. Greedy in the best possible sense; for life, observed, pinned, transfigured and remade.'

— **Keiran Goddard,** *Votive*

'Quill's poetry takes us on a literary journey into a dreamlike underworld, where only the deepest roots of nature will steady us. As our world flounders, this is a resonant and powerful debut.'

— **Jennifer Edgecombe,** *The Grief of the Sea*

'Sam Quill's poetry is taut, formally accomplished and incandescent with rage. 'And / what can history do but turn itself in?', he writes, and makes of that neither a rhetorical nor an open question, but the starting point for a probing and intelligent cross-examination of 'the sense that things are things, and matter'. To compel without chivvying, to be dense without being overloaded, to cry out against abuses (as in the ambitious long poem MILLENIUM: A Vision of Europe) without barking at the moon: this is the good stuff, for heavens' sake get in on it.'

— **John Clegg,** *Pinecoast*

HEY HO THE WHITE SWAN BY GOD I AM THY MAN

Quill

ISBN: 978-1-915079-02-2

Cover designed by Aaron Kent

Edited and typeset by Aaron Kent

Broken Sleep Books Ltd
Rhydwen,
Talgarreg,
SA44 4HB
Wales

Contents

'Nay,' said I, 'I come not from heaven, but from Essex.'
— *A Dream of John Bull*, William Morris

HEY HO THE WHITE SWAN BY GOD I AM THY MAN

Sam Quill

Bark

If I am as strange
as a tree's dream of itself
when we are in bed remember
that I am hewn of timber,
timely and unsafe
as the wood in the wood henge.

Scholastics

The lean's familiar: it is not into the bar
but the world's resistance that he leans; craving
the press of its oak in his ribs, like a lover
in sleep. Only now it's the wind
propping him steady: the good wind at his back.

There, the castle craggies at the sky
and after the sky, Snowdonia.

He thinks about Klee's angel first, then
of something Benjamin wrote later, in France;
and in and through these thoughts he can't remember
the place and hour of his birth. (It troubles me.

This is no port to sail from. I know
that I came among things unresisted.
Ever since I've found the way they fall,
slighted by touch, like a baby's skull,
a grievous curse.)

                  His hair whipped into curls
that whip his ears, his teeth no good,
for prophecy,
              he leans into the storm,
watches the castle ruin itself, there!

It is not into the wind but the world's resistance,
that, and the bar's safe oak.

Damnatio Memoriae

This has nothing to do with politics
but when I think of thousands of statues falling
into deep snow, by one, by two, by three,
some felled together, comradely, and some
in sterile isolation, I am happy.

And when I think of what happened to Sejanus,
his sick ambition thumbed from the used coins;
and of the thousand pyres that burned John Wycliffe;
and of Hemingway's brain, under the cosh of electric
and the cosh of wine and the bullet's blackening cosh;
and all that Anne Frank managed to forget, I am calm.

I am given comfort by the thought
of locust plagues, the flooding of museums;
the image of a drowned man who is pinned
beneath a waterfall, never to surface;
and, yes, the burning of books.

Aeneid (1)

— From Book II

Mrs Dalloway said she would gather the limbs of Osiris herself

Someone is always missing
and most of the time
it is one of the Gods. Ceres, who,
since my earliest visions of Love,
I (who was a pious child)
have known to resemble my mother,
was not in the place that was holy to her alone
when we came looking. It was me who carried the prince,
my father's, weight; lugged him on my back,
cushioned with a lion's hide
so that my labour and his ride was easy.

Someone is missing, always:
I am missing, every day, the fortunate tide;
Retiarius casts his net and is missing.

But nothing missing is absent. It is not loss
but the fact that in our misses we are made
by our Gods to watch a universe displacing,
which upsets us. And
that the knowledge of what might have been is public,
is a kind of humiliation.

This is why we ask: 'Why am I here?'
Which is not hypothetical:
fully distilled, it means: 'Why am I not there?'
It is why I could not leave the house today.
It is why I cannot go to bed
till I have wished a real goodnight
to real Aeneas in my bronze,
among the other, glassy shades.

But I will speak a tonight about what happened
when we left Troy at last
and certainly for good.

I said that she was missing, but the truth
is she was left behind. I had my father,
on my back, and in my hand
our son, Ascanius, who was
tripping a little ahead of me. I had
been up all night, fighting something or other,
and we'd said goodbye already, so I thought.

They had given me, with certain drugs
to ease our parting, a black flower;
I kept it with me, crushed it in my pocket.
At midday as we nursed our pints of bitter,
weak enough to gentle us half-way
into the future, at a table outside The Bear,
I saw (or thought I saw, at first;
then remembering the memory that ghosts
have been with me a while, knew I saw)
Creusa, in the sun on Blue Boar Lane.

We both knew I'd be there.

When I offered her my flower she did not take it,
knowing that then, nor now, a decade later,
it would not mean a thing once I was sober.

And so I tried, knowing she would not kiss me,
being vaster than I was, and built like a god,
to hug her. She held me steady,
moving, still, away. So I stood up
and tried again to hold her. She held me, then,
as friends would hold me soon, commiserating.
Then: *well, third time lucky!* I threw myself
at the air just where my slow eyes thought she stood.

Once they'd picked me up she was long gone.

It is hard to be exiled
on the maelstrom
of a pint's dregs.
Sink! Sink! and among that, a last order:

Desist, my much-lov'd lord, 't indulge your pain;
You bear no more than what the gods ordain.

An Understanding

after Cavafy

My strung-out adolescence, its senseless
devotion to the sensual life… well:

I came to my senses and by way of them
to its sense, which is clear as settled ale.

There are good things in the waiting.
This proves my dream of futility

futile, my practice of mannered apologia, itself
a sorry state of affairs. How was I to know?

When I was a wet (deep in those years
of lager-sweats and fags behind the ears)

my poems got a feel for the forms they desired.
This is why all my sorrys were unstable, and my pledges

to restrain myself (who had so much to restrain)
lasted a fortnight, tops.

Two Rivers

at the confluence of the Rheidol and the Ystwyth at the Irish Sea

Two rivers: one is pinned at its mouth by a tide,
the other insists itself brackishly into the waves.
Violence comes and goes. A snowy shiv
of spindrift spittle quivers like a tilde

above that primal, almost-hominid vowel
which oceans break us with, below the blare
of easy water; heard with a full skull,
beyond the grammar of the inner ear.

Talk in town says that a yearling otter
has made this stretch its home. I dread to think
of the beast tonight; somehow colder, wetter
than its genes promised. (I'm wrong, of course. The drink

is its to live in, ours to sink and fear.)
At this late angle, moonlight warms the crest
of each black wave through lengths of matted air
only as sunlight dazzles the cold east

of Neptune on the better days of its Spring.
There's something about here that's not about here.
Mars has gone to war tonight. A gang
of dolphins leaps in darkness, somewhere near.

Litany

When the room and my bathwater settled at last on a temperature they could both stomach,
I knew (if I wanted to lose the more miserable parts of an already miserable evening) I needed
some air before darkness.

So leaving a can which agreed with my bathwater as to the temperature needed to shift my inertia,
I set out to breathe
in the air before darkness,

then pissed out an hour in search of my shoes and concluding *I won't give up smoking.*
It was late, too late, when I picked up the pouch of tobacco whose fumes I imagined would sweeten the air
in the air before darkness,

and maybe it was for that reason alone that this evening I broke with all habit and turned from the heavier waters that churn up
the beach to the finer more delicate mists that are sweated by waters when they go to town.
(The difference is less in the state of the matter, than some metaphysical sleight which to serious tongues tells of too little salt
in the air before darkness.)

Pushing through dusk-feathers, strewn in the alleyways, seeking St. Michael's. I climbed up the tower
and watched myself walk on the beach
in the air before darkness,

already too steeped
in the air before darkness.

And when, at last, I made it home after all of ten minutes and decades of plausible years,
I met myself crossing the threshold and said to myself, 'Did you see what I saw
In the air before darkness?'

'No!' I replied. You'll forget what I've told you
since both of us swore not to speak more than once (can you hear me?)
of air before darkness.

One-Time Pad

after Cavafy

He made, once, a poem unlike his others.
He did not write it down; no need,

it was, after all, already made of memory,
so tempered to the worldly notes it sung,

as if (*as if*, he liked that part) the day-bright earth
were a wine glass made to hum, under the feather – the eagle's feather! –

of his spread-feathering hand. To give it even the ghost's body of Word
would be to bring his wax too close the the fire, to learn,

by a method that seemed depressing French, that the essence of a thing
is nothing without its formal particularities, its taste

in the head. Better not risk all that.
So, when he read, he would read other poems. To him, it made no odds

whether he read for a crowd or to himself (aloud
or in his head), or whose name took the credit.

They were all unlike the poem that was unlike
his others, and which he did not write

down. One night, when we were in bed, and hadn't fucked
for a week, he told me, I don't know why, about the poem,

then told me every word. I have used every word a thousand times
and in a thousands orders, even today, which is a day

on which I did not write. He tells me, when we speak, which isn't often,
that he cannot remember the poem now, but is happy, regardless, to know

that he, perhaps, has recited it unawares,
while he told me the tale of his latest, terrible love.

Deor

Þæs ofereode | þisses swa mæg (Deor, anon.)

Weland knew serpents, how they bit and killed.
He stood his ground; he had known harder things.
He missed friends, mostly, and the winters got to him:
their *wintery* cold. His luck was bad
when he fell into debt with Nitðhad,
and being, as he said, the bigger man,
he worked it off. It took him twenty years.
As that passed, so may this.

When her brothers died, Beadohild was pregnant,
so she found it hard to concentrate on grief.
She found it hard, too, to think of the baby.
As that passed, so may this.

You'll have heard about Mætðhilde,
so hard in love, poor girl, she couldn't sleep.
As that passed, so may this.

Theodric ran the city of the Mærings
for thirty years. He was famous, known.
As that passed, so may this.

Of Eormanric's wolfish mind
we all know too well. He ruled the Goths
with grim kinging! They could only *wish* him gone.
As that passed, so may this.

Men lose their sprits. Men give up the ghost. *God knows
what's next*, they say, *God knows what's next.*

I want to tell you something about myself.
I was a poet, looked after for a while by the Heodenings.
I loved them, I was good to them. My name was Deor.
But now Heorrenda, a hustling man
who reads with impressive charisma,
has taken my job and leaves me nowhere to live.

As that passed, so may this.

MILLENNIUM: *A vision of Europe*

Someone once said that it is easier to imagine the end of the world than to imagine the end of capitalism. We can now revise that and witness the attempt to imagine capitalism by way of imagining the end of the world.

— Frederic Jameson, 'Future City' in *New Left Review*

I. THE TRIUMPH OF THE SUN

This late radicalization of the moon,
its libertine
detachment, is the six times spangled banner
on the lunar
surface
solar-blasted white. Disgrac
-ing gift, star-bleaching star: Helios.
Reflect on the reflected lawlessness
of sunflowers and on the fix of paint,
their remedy. The deadname of the light
and the name of the birth thing
that is what it is, wholly. Flung
into the cornea's deep field.
Undead.
Son of the weird reaches of the black
and still farther, clock
me at my speed:
do you read
me?
The light is rose and I am out of time.

II. NOVEL

Beyond crosscurrent,
the whole belligerent
cries into a health-winded night
                                        and makes it rain
on the deliberate Aegean.
Austere demos,
remorseless
in unwelcome,
shifts the scene of European crime
uneasily in box-fresh jackboots
and frets
about its kind and commonweal.
The vision is unhealthy. Hostile,
even, as in

the breakers' equine vocation,
the hand that draws
white water. Breaking a horse
in. Hectoring
with the whip-hand and running
sore.

Ancestral houses, predicating war
on funereal
waters, slick with the shades of oil
and occasional fire.
                        St. Helena
cresting, as if it were
an eagle.
            Napoleon is silent.
He moves us to America.
                            Its stunt
of culture is a blessing
to the jawing
Jacobin in the cornmarket
with his undarned stockings, cut
pages and uncombed hair.

America is never.

We share
this soliciting hour
with Sabha's slave market
and with the ships off Al Khoms,
                              now cresting too,
                                        now paling with the bucket,
calling out the holy form of the mountaintop, and
speaking an uncertain mind
in the waveforms
                    of Proteus.

Napoleon is
in the Bastille and there is blood
on the streets of Paris. Blood
on the curb at Marseille.
Blood,
          say:

Yet he shall come to his end, and none shall help him.

It is safe to say
                    this time
that Albion is dead
                    not sleeping. His bowel
picked over by a chalky-white gull
on Whitstable beach. Alone
and without company,
                    he noses the grit,
                              celebrating communion
with his flesh in the revolting provinces of his flesh
and catching suddenly now
                    on the extreme lash
of my eye

is a hilltop within distant sight of Coventry.
High days of December. A lungful of moon
in the shriving sun
and a folly erected in mushy woodland
                              to the slaughter
of the king's favourite

          In Life and Death,
          A memorable Instance of Misrule.

                    ~

I am a mouse
crushed between the leaves
of my seventeenth-century grammar,
where
the eye levels with itself in a longer view
and all of our knowers must know
the singularity of their knowledge,
                  how it scribes
and circumscribes
with a single hand.

And
what can history do but turn itself in,
incline
in the pastoral
way of tendril
and vine, on the familiar branches
and the blood of the happy tree?
                  Winter dispatches
and promises
because the shepherds' calendars say so.
Come,
I have briefed against them.

III. The Fifth Monarchy

Plough bare bones
then wait for rain. Unfailing life declines
the verbs which are its regular gift. And scholarship is
a fold of the vision.
                    Bless.

In the affairs of state, material
is shiftless. To get word of the real
hold out for it: belly sounding the dust,
nails clawing for the fitting object. To persist
in a processional grammar is
to see things proselike, when God knows what is
coming:
triumph not movement; song,
perhaps.

Among the rutty turnips
and the blight
I have seen
                    infinity in a hazelnut,
becoming flesh of apostate and soldier. Not metamorphosis
but substance cleaving on substance
in the troughs and crowns of unperfected years,
before a prophet was turned.
                            They cropped his ears
and he took the holy brand.

He went with his heat
                            at the angels who would not rescind
their unmade oath, first torture; with his flush and his flame.

His men are my sad saints. Their timely dream
will bring them to heaven in the villages
and in the ports and fields; bald-bellied sages
who have seen their God
and know that he is good.

Happy are those
                    who smile to see that Isis
feeds the crop, that the Great Ouse,
the Blackwater and Severn,
brain their banks against the sculling flood.
                                        Here a storm drain
breaches; where I step

the earth is bodied full. Oceans grow steep,
impassable. Now the water table is upturned

$\qquad\qquad\qquad\qquad\qquad\qquad$ and this tide's feast
is the last.

A strong and stable bleed
irrigates the dry bones of the dead.

The event horizon
$\qquad\qquad\qquad$ passed us by—
you did not notice.
Here we can move only and directly
towards the singularity,
into its song
$\qquad\qquad$ and here there is just movement
without counting; the terror of the firmament
is here.

And here
(world without end)
$\qquad\qquad\qquad\qquad$ at the world's end
the wind
rises as a single horn
in the weather's turbine.

Through its pipe
$\qquad\qquad\qquad$ I say:
Things cannot be

shut up in finite revolutions.

Begins
the sky
pitching into celebrant velocity,
where speed on speed
$\qquad\qquad\qquad\qquad$ will transubstantiate
and heavy, heavy, heavy
$\qquad\qquad\qquad\qquad$ is the lime light
and the gold.

I.V. i. m. NERO

At times like these
I think aways
of the corals of Antarctica,
of snow, colder than water,
falling through water and falling out of light.
Of flakes quenching in the burning chill, in the octopus blot
of deep and southern oceans; on the crests
of underwater mountains, falling into flooded caves.
Of the human silence of the lifting sea

dies with me, dies with me, dies with me.

V. THE SECOND TRIUMPH OF THE SUN

Still, not yet quite wholly out of mind
                            among all this
he lies
on the lip of the deliberate Aegean.

Alan Kurdi.
            Not the first to drown.

Whose lungs give amp and throttle to the howl
that goes up through Europe,
                            for a while
goes up through Europe, stirring
the Reichstag and the Palace of Westminster, fueling
the newsfeeds
            and Grub Street in their ravenous turns?

Say:
    He will be kinged in the crowning of a thousand Suns.

No, it cannot be that.
                    Once more, try
this:
    No remedy.

(I will concede it here,
these politics are
no more than a death wish.
I will not live again, millennial. Crush
me. Let me make way.)

~

Hard by the Door of the Sun
                        and in the Sun's own key
I have have heard
                torturer twining victim
in piano wire.

Loud-hailing choir,
calling to my mind
                    one particular netsuke
In the British Museum: cut of ivory
in a hand of Tadamasa.
A bodhisattva,
named Kannon in their catalogue.

Ride with him on the haunches of the lion dog,
who is wailing his law
into the missionary cosmos. It is a kind of flair.

Ask what gives
to be elect in his company, whose
reason leads you hardly now
                              into the still birthing Sun.

The light that shone
in the axel tree is dying.
The light that was burning
in the dawn at London Fields,
turned through the branches
if the happy tree,
is dying. O my gallows-tree,

it is noon
and the weird Sun in the blockchain
holdsfast.

The first
death is never enough.
I believe

in the end of the world.

Thinking Stepped Into Me On Lambeth Bridge

And though I had walked for years that night, it wasn't
the sort of night that settles the usual questions,
being those of love and territory, upon

the neurons' cartogram. I did not quarter
the citadel into its heavenly quarters;
no angels danced in Islington or Peckham.

It was a kind of trial: licks of flame
then coals beneath me on the glacial pavement
that burned like tinnitus. Do not imagine

more emptiness than fell between my steps
on Lambeth Bridge. From Lambeth Bridge I turned
east, so that I stood across the river

from Parliament, sitting very late.
There would be news; the lower house was pulsing
through its lobbies. I didn't stick around.

Get out of here. Get out. Get out. There is,
spawned in the low tide, a kind of snake
that breathes and spasms while it lies in wait,

and winter of some kind to be endured
in any case. I went instead to Queenhithe
and thought of Queen Mathilda until dawn.

'A San Isidro'

after Calderón

My life in the sky
burns its copy
into dumb plazas
while the shamed angels

agree that both
red soil and blithe
swifts can teach
so much, so much.

Sky-labourers, early
to love and holy
singing, know
by heart the new

sweetness of prayer;
God does not care,
and the tear's bead
is a fertile seed.

My labouring angel,
living a double
life will exhaust
your burning dust,

don't be afraid
of lights that guide
your eye from the light
and sow tears, the fruit.

Endurance: Holy Week

for Sarah

A parliament is choiring in her nerves.
   It finds its crises most reliably
at the census-taking. One by one, her doves

   return from the hard country, ecstatically
cooing about a goodlife that persists
   in those abolished regions. She could die

for some good news. An ashen feather drifts
   into her palm, she shivers while it shivers:
blueing and whiting like her blue-white wrists.

   I pity the song of the angelic orders
which inculcates her into downy grief
   for what they made her flesh.
                                        But her wings' feathers

will be hewn of rich, enduring stuff,
   of kevlar-diamond; which become the smile,
which is the resurrection and the life.

Lucre

I dreamed about the inventory of Rembrandt
the bankrupt's house.
How everything was costed (even the Porcellis)
because he was in debt.
We can't, he says,
understand,
less settle the whole estate
with light ripped from another artist's mind.

Today I can remember Amsterdam,
its wine traders,
and the exotic names of its even its poorest burghers,
because in the worst dream
that night conjures,
she belongs,
not here but in its time,
is living always among Rembrandt's things.

Why do I dream her into that low brown,
that canal light?
It is something to do with the weird,
erotic nature of debt and of things we own,
how the freight
of that whole crime
cannot be told or shown,
as if to tell were somehow to redeem.

Firedream on Tan y Bwlch

Alone in all this peace and wild,
town, I'd tell you (should we meet,
which we will not) was revealed
twice to me, in a dream I met

after thirteen days awake…
'A town of folded golden paper,
where there was no light: I struck
a match to glimpse it in the taper:

thus I burned it to the ground.
Town's now brighter than the flame
I'd torched it with. (This, the second
image worrying my dream

is worse, forgive me). The sad truth
is that beneath the summer's light
nobody's healthy. If you breathe
at all, breath air half-salt, half-wet;

(here I'd gesture to the surf
which has grown wilder, closer) air,
which won't confess your half-belief
in anything resembling fire.

Draughts of heaven (listen, stranger)
burned just like the draughts of hell.'
You are not with me. I remember
now that I have not been well.

Alone in all this peace and wild,
town is where it seems to be:
braced against a slighted world,
and a still, collapsing sea.

Turning home, how could I grieve
for mermen in their coralled beds?
Harbouring myself, I leave
the sea to tear itself to shreds.

The Ship of Theseus

Each night was the same, or seemed to be
a mirror of its ancestors, only
the casks a little emptier at closing
until new stock came in. One day the brassy
handle on the gents began to lose
some of its lustre. Nothing much at first
but after a while the sort of touch the landlord
didn't care for. so he got a new one.
After that the red paint on the walls
began to chip and scuff and darken slowly
until I saw the tannins in its wine.
They gave the place a lick of paint and no one
spoke of it again. But things kept going,
and after that moved noticeably quickly.
First the wear on the tables disappeared,
the red upholstery lost its stench of wind,
and every day the windows let more light in.
The beers turned over at unlikely speeds
and were changed like for like. Once I was sure
that the paintings on the walls had been replaced
by perfect copies of themselves, made over.
The punters never seemed to age at all.
Each year they were refreshed. The same clothes
and familiar names having the same conversations,
those dying generations at the bar.
One August night, I noticed that the clock
was striking eleven again: then I knew
that I had never been inside that pub.
I used to drink in The Ship of Theseus.

The Lost Decade

you know who you are

Paris ten years ago was something else.
I have a photograph but I have lost
the way to feel it, even the hit of pain
that drives the homing pigeons to their nests
in Saint-Denis. I know a river too,
each day it drags its haul far out to sea
and atrophies at Sheppey and at Grain.
September's on the still length of the river.
I have never stepped into its source
nor seen the stretch where miles of abstract water
bloom into grey oceans. Nor, I think,
till now, have I set eyes on it in months.

Still there somehow and having never left
are those I never left and left, somehow
forever. Let them persevere in light
that is still light in me though here the clouds
accrue like lipids in an engorged liver:

Christ help me. And his father. And his ghost.

In the neutral morning they'll be waking now,
ten years ago, and as they wake they'll notice
the staining of the air by light diffused
through air, as through cold water, green pastis.
They will hear of the death of Juan Almeida
on the radio and very far away.
We did things like that then and things went on
like that until they didn't. Only now
is the hush that followed audible, and now
does absence become real as time unloved.

Things went on that way till Halloween.
There was a red hotel, a bed, a final day
and a liqueur cabinet. (It makes me happy
always to describe the things we drank,
so bear with me: there was, for red, a spoiling
Pinot Noir that bit my lip and gargled;
and then a Muscadet and some warm beers
which looked into a mirror at each other,
each wanting the other more than it wanted itself;
and after that, as afternoon wore blank,
whisky.) It was time to for us to leave.

From the red room we walked, from the hotel
then through that evening's valium's dustbath
to Gallieni, for the London coach.
And I told you that story with Fitzgerald:

how he knew he'd never be happy again,
or not so happy, never quite so happy.

Yes, I knew exactly what I did.

We are stirring in the wash close to Embankment,
rousing in the mud like drowsy babies
who once were slipped some cognac in their milk
then slept almost forever. Leave us for dead.
Sprawled on the mudflat, moony throats aspiring
to things that might excuse us. Excuse me.

The lost decade will host us on its terms.

Loved aporia, grow in me day by day
like a troubling cell's fractal malignity;
uncreative, or spawning only your likeness.
Already now, on the shrill banks of the Thames
are hundreds and hundreds of birds, already here
and hundreds more are descending. Noon is gone
and as the herons come the sky will darken
into its perfect, equitable black,
knowing only that it was for this.

Aeneid (2)

— From Book IV

Mars, it's you; I know that chin,
rising through puny wars. It bloodied,
when I was a refugee, scree off the rig
till I stung with more than tears. Salted
lips that kissed Aeneas; reddy lips
whose ghost licks salt. I am sorry.

Not you rising: I am falling.
That burn is my pyre;
the smoldering flesh of Dido, Queen of Carthage.
I want to see the plants my ashes sow in heaven.

It is cold now, deathly cold;
self-arsoned body settles with the night.
I know where we are. Hell, beneath
the spun wool of my smock, smolders; this earth
is not your earth, not mine. It is hard forever.

Three months settled me. I saw you coming
down an escalator at St. Pancras station,
with the look of a man who did not want to see me.
Your hair washed in the essence of its essence, dyed
in all the refining shades of prophecy. So dark
the whites of my eyes vanished.
It was you, with gods to tell me about gods
and how they worked you. Here, you speak:

'Dido, it's you; I know. Nothing is sacred.
But in the grave… listen:
above us spheres churn, rocks bleed
through sister rocks, like we bled through our mothers.
Nothing is guilty of killing.
Me, you and your knife: conspiracy.
The flames: disposal of a body. Mud
eats only what it has. This turns my stomach
which makes a kind of fantastic music.

The grave has a sacred thing
now that you're dead, being my sacrifice.

I don't know about Fate,
but because I have her promise I can smile,
meeting you, even here, half dead,
and looking worse than you have ever seen me. Ignore
the sick on my trousers, the Malbec on my shirt.
This place is new to you. I know it well.
The grave has a sacred thing, which is its promise.'

At the sound of 'sick', I stopped
and turned, not having it now and wanting enough,
towards a brighter, warmer bit of hell.

He said: 'What don't you want to know?
I'll take myself for now,
but I can't take the feeling that I was,
or will be, when you think of Aeneas again;
in a devil's arms, warm arms.

And this is what I meant by 'Fate'. A joke:
it's the best of all possible underworlds, I love it.
Suffer meeting me here, sick. Dido, Fate has promised
that this will come to good. I know you saw Mars burning.
I set the fires that put you here. I set
your body in the flesh of Pygmalion.'

The Sea and the Mirror

No wind, no bother. Dusk. The sea
reveals a sensitivity
to each tired photon's twilight year;
takes them in its fretless care,

till morning. For this sacrifice
of intimacy, asks a price:
it wants to know the daylight's hand.
Rumours pass like contraband

from the exiled starlight to
the blacklists of surveilling blue.
Tomorrow when the first lights seep
out of the double-blinded deep,

the sea will know to pose the feather
of each wave to suit the weather.
Thank the sea, which will not shatter
your sense that things are things, and matter.

Acknowledgements

I would like to thank my editor, Aaron Kent, for his courage, patience and skill; also, for their help in drafting these poems, Sarah Fletcher and Patrick Davidson Roberts.

LAY OUT YOUR UNREST